PRAISE

These provocative, trustworthy poems owe their strength
to narrators who are not afraid to confront their own
sense of awe, misgivings, and incredulity, as it pertains
to their various stations in life. The prevailing subject
of parenthood, and what it means to shepherd children
through the stages of growth, keeps circling in this
superb collection—none more so than in "The Perfect
Dad." Long before this final section, however, we
witness personal journeys towards reconciliation and
how to parent not only a child, but also humankind, on
a practical, universal level. *Cupping Our Palms* has a
stirring habit of casting its readers far out into a sea of
curiosity and wonder, and, then, rather methodically,
reeling or easing its audience back to shore, turn
by gradual turn, through its eloquent language and
structural change of pace. Compelling as "Beacons of
Light," "Not for Sale," "Parabolic," and "Relics" appear,
they're gateways to more profound questions the poet
addresses and destiny poses, to all readers. Yes, here are
rich, haunting poems, replete with honest voices whose
declarations linger, long after the collection is complete—
lessons well learned—but never quite at rest.

—Bart Edelman, 2022 Birdy Poetry Prize Judge,
Whistling to Trick the Wind

A sidelong glance at America in a sallow heartless corruptive age, kept hopeful by wise lines that push against the darkness like fireflies in the night. Boll weevils, Kardashians, Whitman, the 1%, a hit job in Jersey and a precious sick child reside amicably and awkwardly together in the way the best art does—startling us into new insights into who we would like to be, and who we decidedly don't want to be. Greenhause's work is wry and knowing, but not too cool for its own humanity. Perhaps most critically of all, these finely wrought poems pass a simple, underrated test: you want to keep reading them, and gladly.

—Joe Hoover, S. J., Editor, *America*

Cupping Our Palms

Winner of The Birdy Poetry Prize—2022
by Meadowlark Press

CUPPING OUR PALMS

poems by
JONATHAN GREENHAUSE

Meadowlark
PRESS
Emporia, Kansas, USA

Meadowlark Poetry Press, LLC
meadowlarkbookstore.com
P.O. Box 333, Emporia, KS 66801

Cupping Our Palms
Copyright © Jonathan Greenhause, 2022

Cover Design: TMS, Meadowlark Press

Cover Photo: Jonathan Greenhause

Author Photo: Raquel D'Apice

Interior Design: Linzi Garcia, Meadowlark Press

ISBN: 978-1-956578-19-5
Library of Congress Control Number: 2022943063

I've been blessed with 2 exemplary fathers in my life: One—Richard Friedman—who raised me, and the other—Rosario D'Apice—who raised my wife. *Cupping Our Palms* is dedicated to my father-in-law, who passed away on July 18th , 2022.

If there's a heaven, Ross is there, chatting with everyone about how lucky he was; and they, in turn, are extremely lucky to have him, as he deserved every bit of his good fortune.

From one of your honorary sons: I love you. We miss you.

CONTENTS

I. Everything, for a Reason

II. To Sugarcoat the Truth

III. The Perfect Dad

I. Everything, for a Reason

Circles

"Try it again," she whispers, as I pick through the fish's bones
at this beachside stand equipped with full bar

within earshot of a drum circle. Her middle-aged skin's
sunburnt, as she burns through her savings

to lessen her sea-soaked guilt. This is 20 years ago
& a dozen kilometers to the south of Tulúm. She swims

in a lukewarm pool of bourbon, her makeup
a personal Guernica, blurred blue eyes the dazzling reflection

of a naked bulb doubling as a commuter train's approach.
Today, I'm the age she was then, my sons dipping

in & out of the Atlantic, eclipsed by waves, miraculously
spit out again. They call & respond, are beaten

& bowled over, tossed like salads, like sailboats by a sea spout
I fail to foresee. "Try it again,"

the absent woman repeats, as I lie by the surf,
trying to write what happened, what I hope will never happen

to mine, am ashamed for not remembering
her exact features, if her eyes were really blue, if she insisted

it may've been an accident, her daughter high
while stumbling along the tracks, a purse with her IDs

flung from the body. Afterwards, I hug the shore for a mile
before finding it: A massive silence punctuated

by an MC Escher sea, black waves lined with white
as they gently roll in, the full moon a Broadway spotlight,

low-flying clouds turning the world on & off—on & off —
as if hatching existence, then drowning it out,

sowing possibility with this fluid truth
that everything's despair, until hope ascends to the surface.

Jonathan Greenhause

The fire-escape,
no longer weighed down

by tomato plants & basil
                lifts up by micro-millimeters towards the sky,
& the sky peers down,   is baffled by the limits
it can & cannot know;   how here it's the sky, but there it isn't,
how a few degrees of air
can lessen into nothing.   Even a fire can wonder what it is,
if it's only the flames   or also the smoke, the heat
dissipating into what may be sky,
into the fire-escape's melted steel,   how two things become one
& how a single thing   is almost never just one substance,
is always a little less or more,
always a metamorphosis
                                between what it was
                                                        & what it'll be.

Staring at the sky & the fire & the fire-escape,
the child only knows   he's a child,
not quite adolescent   yet no longer crawling on all fours.
He knows & doesn't know   how this moment won't ever repeat,
how the smoke   which may
or may not be part of the fire   seeps into his lungs,
& how the fire-escape,   melting
into the fire,   is no longer an escape
but more like the sky,
more like a stretch of nothing   serving no use to him,
all these things inevitably joining
to become one in the same:
                                The boy & the fire,
                                                        the escape & the sky.

On the Road Trip

America, where are you? I've been searching
at shopping malls,

                                        dodging prosecutors

who eye adolescent girls as they sing
the Lord's praises.

                                         I've resorted to verse

to unearth the all-inclusive voice of
Whitman, but it's mute.

                                         Perhaps the highways

might park me near the ghost of Nabokov,
arrest our troubling

                                         Reality phase

of governance. I could check cornfields, sleep
in alleys, hop

                                         on freight trains, mainline

opioids, but corporate interests would keep
your majesty veiled.

                                         As you're wined & dined

by 1%-ers, we'll find America
in our uniqueness,

                                         in what we've become.

Jonathan Greenhause

A poem written in my past life as a 15th-century Georgian monk

wouldn't start off like this,
would be surprised to find itself encaged in English,
penned from the perspective of a 21st-century American.

Everything would be unsettling: The free verse, the
abrupt line breaks, the passing allusion
to the Soviet Union. What's

a Soviet Union? & what's an American?
The poem would invariably question
its own existence, would doubt the veracity of its origins

yet revel in its incongruity, in its
wish to transcend its beginnings. The Georgian monk
would stare back at the page, marveling

at his absurd creation, hardly giving himself time
to let the ink dry; yet every errant word
would discover its place.

He'd come back to the poem,
crafting lines inspired by prayers, or by the lack of them;
& a hole would grow inside of him

greater than the bones strapping it in:
He'd stuff it with orations, with a plunging of his hands
into the soil of the monastery's garden,

digging out roots, ingesting them, then adding a stanza
about the Kardashians, imagining how this praise
would surely please the heavens.

Extant/Extinct

Crush the cockroach but
        not the ant,
not the bees buzzing by

        your palm
about to press into mine,
        not the legs

of centipedes caressing
        concrete,
not Chihuahuas' feet

        resting in
a litter of nine. Trust
        the seal

but not the sliminess
        of eels,
not their slithering lack

        of width,
not the suspect strength
        of their length,

not their tendency
        to bend
into a clandestine dress

        of darkness.
Scrap the European starlings
        shipped to

the Americas, but prevent
the condors
from going extinct. Ensure

the presence
of pheasants, the survival
of crows,

the rows of marshland
heron's nests.
Wrest away the hold of

boll weevils,
the pernicious appetite
of starry

sky beetles, the suffocating
menace
of the zebra mussel.

Tussle
with walruses but not with
wolverines,

not jaguars nor panthers
nor badgers;
& keep track of what's

extant
but soon will likely land on
a longlist

of the regrettably lost,
of what's
sure to be tempest-tossed.

Beacons of Light

"The sea will claim what belongs to the sea," says my son
at age 6. We're steering
a rusted fishing vessel in the middle
of the Atlantic. Cattle soar above us
in a jetliner heading to pastureland. "The sea's
just another word for oblivion," says my son
as he reels in another refugee
& gently hugs her, wraps her in the emergency
Mylar blanket. He pulls out
a cellphone, activates
Google Translate, & the woman's Arabic becomes
"Your President is a vulture with a hunger
for its own eggs," as she pleads
to be taken somewhere else, maybe
Canada. The other refugees
nod their heads, tell tall tales of a distant
Manitoba. "The sea will devour our beacons of light
in their death throes," says my son
as he leaps overboard, dives beneath
the sky's reflection, saves
a small shivering boy barely distinguishable from himself.

Jonathan Greenhause

Sacrifice

The bee stinger's an oil derrick buried in the earth's skin,
a dried-out prick sticking like a briar
into my bare limb, a snapshot of apiary pain
from a camera flashing low on battery. I apply cream,
set her lifeless husk beside
my sugar-stained bottle, my disposable fork repurposed
as tiny hoe to excavate a vault, to honor this shell
believing her aches have purpose,
her plush hairs caressing the potential for heavenly flight.

Bristled legs cling to her belly, like a figure skater's arms
amidst the dizzying swing of centripetal force,
an aging gambler Jonesing for a bit of beginner's luck.
Mad as a mink herd tracked by fur trappers,
the bee ought to have sought to colonize a gentler terrain,
to touch down on a potato patch,
crown herself queen of a pocket park or duke
of a spoiled ham sandwich, regent of a towering field
of zigzagging sunflowers. Instead,

she stepped out of her secretive waggle dance,
declared a blitzkrieg against the ceramic bowl housing
my paprika-battered egg salad,
deserted her younger brethren, her stingless drones
to learn on their own, mistook herself
for a mole, dug in just as I ventured to serve myself up
an insect-free helping, right as she spotted
this would-be aggressor, felt justified to sacrifice herself
for the communal good of whatever evil perceived in me.

The Weight of Your Body

Frost on railroad ties. A squirrel crosses fast
before my terrier spots it, scurries
up an ivy wall, then vanishes. Last
week, your body was found here, blackberries'

vestiges smearing hard soil with its sweet
stain. Police; an ambulance; then silence.
The freight train blasts its horn as we retreat
to a wooded area, my dog's prints

sunk into stiff mud where frogs await Spring.
We hear the ring of church bells, the mating
call of a robin. What were those last few
hours like for you, trembling with cold, a view

of branches intersecting sky? This life
grew on you, but not enough to survive.

Fractaling the Blue

Mushrooms map a Jackson Pollack portrait across a clavicle
polished as if missing from a museum. We sit
with shovels at age 14, brows swim-soaked with sweat
as if we've been plucked
from the public pool, mercilessly bum-rushed
by prepubescent drool. It's summer in a midsized town
in Jersey, & the lush world's encapsulated
within our subdivisioned sight, loosened soil stuck to skin
like sand grains at the tide's line
or oil slicks adhered to seagulls at the site
of Exxon's spill in Prince William Sound, its coastal stone
blackening like basalt, mimicking
tarred lungs left breathless. I'm at the dizzying precipice
of adolescence, this pit the perfect size of me
to vault within. Clamoring down its uneven sides,
my slim fingers clutch at severed roots
& a squirming of earthworms, as I crouch within the shadow
of what we've dug, my friend above
silhouetted like an angel, branches crisscrossed
like spiderwebs fractaling the blue. Skeletons' scattered bones
—one by one—are tossed into the light
like stunned visitors emerging from a languorous sleep
destined to break, as my foot gets caught on a splinter
of calcium carbonate, the earth
stabbing its sirens' pleas into my untrained ears
as if here's where time—at last—will freeze its spinning hands.

Everything, for a Reason

The diagnosis of Multiple Sclerosis.
His war in Afghanistan, the flak jacket useless
in warding off the persistence
of night sweats. Your mother, cancerous,

knocking at the Stage IV door. Your rent
fattened, as if by lard. That seagull bent
to pick at fried chicken, foraging
for its fledglings, their warped wings wishing

for gentle landings. If you hadn't done this
or hadn't done that, you wouldn't have
your children. You'd be the run-on sentence
deprived of its chatty prisoners, the laugh

turned genocidal, the pig slipped through a gate
where slaughter's fate still greets it.

Jonathan Greenhause

My father's across the Atlantic, on the verge

of death, & I'm stuck at a travel agency
frantically attempting
to get back home to him. It's mid-May 2001

in Strasbourg, a few blocks
from where the city's Jews were shepherded away
on Valentine's Day

in 1349, some nine-hundred of us
footing the plague's bill
for superstition & ill-will. Imagine their thoughts

while being steered
out of Strasbourg, then subsequently chained
within a wooden house

rotting in the rural Alsatian outskirts, where
they were burnt alive. I, too,
seek a means of escape, a saving-grace

flight back to Jersey,
but this travel agent beaming back at me
rejects my credit card,

triumphantly announces: "Sorry, we don't accept
American Express,"
as my father resists in a hilltop hospital

where I was born
two decades earlier. I sprint between travel agency
& subsidized student apartment,

between scattered homes of friends formed
in this two-month stay,
my red-hot bootsoles birthing blisters

allergic to skin, my lungs
burning as if that Jewish bonfire were still blazing,
history fast-forwarding

to claim another one of its descendants;
but I'm out of time,
flash back to frantic e-mails, my dad's stroke

striking both sides
of his cerebellum. For 8 hours I'm off-balance
between Paris & Newark

with no way of knowing if I'll arrive too late.
From this vantage point,
this purgatory masquerading as the present,

everything appears to be
so insignificant, the sea's towering waves
flattened, our cities

razed, our heritages & inheritances wiped out.
So what will happen
when I touch down at the airport, when

I make contact with the ground, when I bow
to kiss it, to properly
bless this life, unaware of what awaits us?

Jonathan Greenhause

Animal House

A dolphin back-flips in the bathtub, sardines circle in the sink,
a boa's curled around the shower rod,
& a troupe of capuchin monkeys claim ownership
over our medicine cabinet. Up & down the hall,
cheetahs sprint, as a polar bear snacks on salmon in our fridge
& penguins stake out the freezer. Our master bedroom's
host to mating season, to shrill peacocks
showing off, caribou locking horns, sea lion bulls
shoving aside their blubbering competitors. Satin sheets
get overrun by a snake den's slithering warmth,
walk-in closets become caves for a colony of vampire bats
bloodthirstily swinging from hangers,
our wooden walls now windows through which termites chow,
& the dining room's a carnivore's delight,
a place where prey fear to go; while lions, wolves, & crocodiles
patiently wait beside the algae-addled swimming pool.
Regardless of our apartment's rare amenities,
no buyer seems interested, & our pets, too,
an apathetic dog & apoplectic cat,
are no fonder of our menagerie, prefer the dullness
of our back-porch, from which they stare at the advancing sea.

Thanks a lot, Shakespeare, for the Starling

The window, single-paned to preserve not heat
    but historical significance,
presses down upon the simple plank preventing it from shutting;
& in that humble rectangular board
exists a hole through which reasoning escapes, a metallic
accordion-like tube stretching from the dryer's back end
    to the aperture
where the starling enters, where it places twig after twig
to construct a metaphor for impracticality & absurdity,

a snapshot of modern life & our climatic uncertainty,
like building a home on the rim of a smoldering caldera,
its flimsy walls trembling. In 1890, 60 starlings
    were released in Central Park
by the American Acclimatization Society
because Shakespeare made mention of them in *Henry IV, Part I*,
wrote "Nay, I'll have a starling shall be taught to speak
nothing but Mortimer, and give it to him to keep his anger
    still in motion."

By the play's end, the battle rages on, the Hundred Years' War
still unresolved; Now we've got over 200 million starlings
    in North America:
My wife & I let this one stay. We hang wet clothes
upon the backs of chairs, upon our shower rod. We learn
to harness solar energy, to scrap these modern conveniences,
teach our 2 sons to appreciate the subtle rumblings
of an egg set to crack, of a fledgling poised to press its luck
    upon the ledge.

Prayers in the Darkening Woods

We inscribe this box with joyousness, infuse it with rose petals
& the barely-palpable essence of ether,

our tiniest son hanging his flimsy fingers upon its edges
& raucously swinging like an orangutan

'til he slips with his grape-jam silliness to the rotting leaves
of a November-fattened floor.

This is our hidden fount of miracles: A bald spot in a back alley
of a nipped forest, this tucked-away

semiurban gift sacrificing itself to the city's eager barbers,
our palms engrossed in chopping into bits

what persists as gorgeous, what fits into our lonesome pockets.
We sprinkle graham crackers upon dirt

to thwart the thought of famished beasts preying on the lost,
on bar-dazed congregants praying

to be found at last. We tender this thicketed mass upon anyone
who elects to detect it, our moss coats

blanketing stone, our hoarse voices like bells knelling, our vision
blinded by a golden star half-devoured

by the swaying tree-line. Let's delight in this flickering firepit
raging beneath us, marshmallows

offered up to damnation to be alchemized, to sweetly adhere
to our twisted tongues calling out a response.

II. To Sugarcoat the Truth

Aquariums, Westman Islands & Elsewhere

My son's locked in an amorous stare with a beluga whale,
drool slipping like sugar-water from his parted lips
as the Icelandic guide
describes the far-off provenance of our cetaceous guest,
the light fixture's fluorescent glare
flickering like a horror flick's warning to flee;
but these fins & fluke
have nowhere new to swim to,
no Mid-Atlantic feeding spree, no breeding colony
with which to indiscreetly cavort. My son
edges closer, soft nose pressed against the sheet plastic
as he unwittingly lures his aquatic counterpart
with his toddling cuteness, his wide-eyed wonder
reeling in this good-natured prisoner.

                                        Somewhere else
shielded far from our eyes, a small boy
teeters on an artificial strip of land, his salted skin
sunburnt, no family in tow. He lacks the words
to communicate his panic,
his abrupt detachment from kin. Rising up on all sides,
acrylic walls are skillfully engineered
to ward out saltwater. Scraps of rotting food
lay untouched at his soil-stained feet, raw chunks
of red meat, heaps of processed grains. He's greeted
every 20 minutes by a new pod
of gregarious Beluga whales, grinning, chattering in awe.

Descent

Their window's the shape of a child, the sunset
an archer scorching concrete
                                      who targets

panes of streaked glass, a splintering frame eased
upwards, as he waits awe-mouthed for a breeze.

We're cattle, tongues lolling as we swish our tails,
our newbie skins
                        swimming in shadow,

approaching as if string-pulled, a magic show
of conjuring, fingers slipping along a sill

harboring dust from lack of rain. One of us
pokes out his head, the torso
                                      like a tortoise

jutting from the room's shell, sidewalk & street
beckoning 3 floors below; then tragedy's

a top that keeps on spinning, that forgets
how to switch its cycling noise
                                      to quiet.

Jonathan Greenhause

Unwrapped

One day, you run into your childhood
but don't recognize it. You buy it drinks, get it so drunk
it throws up in your new car, paints the upholstery
with the buttered spaghetti & carrots
your mom used to serve you. Later, you run into your childhood,
then back up & run over it again,
making sure it won't return. These gaps in your memory
crumble like potholes in the asphalt
by a seashore undermining you from beneath,
sucking out the names of your long-buried schoolteachers
into the subterranean abyss, erasing every right answer
from Algebra quizzes you aced,
from adolescent dates in gum-plagued cavernous cinemas
where ecstasy depended upon your every right move. Again,
you bump into your childhood
& feel a stir, a knock at your mind's door; so you let it in,
only to hit it over the head & toss it downstairs
into a musty cellar crammed with faded photo albums
& birthday cards from great-uncles and -aunts,
with intricate coin collections worth
nothing more than face value. You're confronted
by the realization your life's finite & soon coming to an end,
so you board up your front door & windows,
flee in panic at a stranger's knocking,
seek shelter in the crowded cellar, where you surround yourself
with voluminous tomes of accumulated text messages;
then you pry open the ornate sarcophagus
whose resident had been hastily enveloped, carefully endeavor
to unwrap your childhood, ask it
for forgiveness, plead that it unravel its secrets; but
beneath the bandages, nothing's there.

Like a Lush

Chairs gaze at each other, glazed in fluorescence.
A buzzing like a convention of bees
clings to the lights, ricochets off miniblinds,
lands in a rush upon the professor's hands

as he flips through sonnets: "This one. These.
Not that." The class are calves struggling to keep up,
are wading through creeks as a flash flood
rumbles into view. Each syllable finds

a zealous adherent, a starved hawk who scans
a bounty hiding in the underbrush,
the lovelorn cricket composing like a lush.
A caretaker cuts the lights by accident,

& we're statues awaiting the sculptor
to bestow us form, a name, whatever we're after.

Slightly Buffetted

Our vehicles are formed of feathers, our mortality rates reduced
by the tenderest collisions. Even our plane crashes

are a coming loose of rubber bands & pine,
every dropped occupant rigged out in recyclable parachutes.

Our flus are a half-dozen sneezes, our measles an opportunity
to connect the dots, our terrorist attacks

witty placards held up demanding justice,
dull cases mired in Appellate Court. Our Climate Change

is theoretical, unable to move the mercury, a horror story
confined to the cinema. We're plagued

by knife-fights traded-in for teaspoons
serving out a choreographed scene of splattered ketchup.

We predictably tire of this safety glut, yearn to be sucked dry
by glamorous vampires, left brainless

by fascist politics, soon stumble upon
the mythic stomping grounds of Ponce de León, surprise him

lounging poolside as he sips a margarita, waves while mouthing
the buoyant lyrics to a Jimmy Buffett tune.

The Bath

At the end, the beginning begins to
      shrink, its faithful details
              blending into

        legend & myth, into a biblical
           morality where God's infallible

but difficult to perceive. The stories
      of genesis & exodus
             soon seize

        this young mother as she fills the bathtub,
          as she cradles her children, starts to scrub

their arms & legs & backs. All is quiet
      in the house, no creaking
           of floors, tiles wet

        as water pushes past the rim. How will
          loved ones react, seeing she was able

to do what she's done? She's perched at the brink
      between proof & doubt,
           doesn't even blink.

Jonathan Greenhause

This Picture-Perfect Precipice

When it pours, our spinning heads
are makeshift umbrellas, our soaked shocks of hair
dripping giddily with sky. We circle like sharks,
like whirling dervishes, the world
slipping away, our unmoored loves devoured
by centrifugal force, by arroyos' flash floods,
by the blinding blasts
of lightning strikes. No motion's more upbeat
than to soar: We flap our leaden arms
expecting they'll be wings, let cyclonic winds
propel us to the edge of this picture-perfect precipice;
while below, the sea swirls
into blotches of oblivion, into the wet dream
of a brush-beaten Van Gogh. To release, to let go
would be to acquiesce,
to deliver ourselves onto the crags & crevices
of misfortune. Instead, let's hurl ourselves
backwards, bestow our trembling lips
with a mouthful of mud, with the bucolic aftertaste
of pastures stained by saltlicks.

Fireflies & Ice Cream

—After Frost

Some say the world will end in fireflies,

        some say in ice cream:

From what I've tasted from the skies,

        I hold with those

    who favor flavors

        like butter-pecan

  or mint to savor;

though thinking back

    on stranger treats,

      a flapping incandescence of the two

might be exact

    in terms of sweet

      to guarantee destruction, too.

Hit at the Jersey Shore, 1985

The carpet's polyester fibers press against
his pockmarked face, the body
a blue-suited landscape of rolling hills
composed of hips & bloated belly, his skin
the calm surface of a pond. We wait
outside this motel room,
a caravan of the displaced, my mother
with preadolescent children in tow, a key
screeching in the lock
busted or stuck, the deadweight of metal
gnawing on metal. Tomorrow we'll wander
to where hypodermic-needles
crash into the Central Jersey shore, waves
setting back sand, breaths mingling
on the chintzy boardwalk. We shift feet
like flamingoes, each new minute
poking a dozen more stars
into the punctured sky. Inside, his body
rests awkwardly between a warped desk
& the slumping bed, will require
3 men to lug it out, the cops
halfheartedly dusting for prints
like kids obliged to polish off their veggies.
A thousand summer nights
will erase all this, will slick our skin
with a black hole's magnetism, will order
a hit down to every last one of our souls,
our brothers & sisters
whacked in their places of work
& in their homes. A hall light flickers,
then gives off sparks
before its cinematic explosion. No one
rushes to witness this epilogue,
this snuffing out. No one really expects
a reprieve. No one will make it out alive.

.he Truth

bad?"

s dense snow falls outside

y in its bed
of autumn leaves. __ father, I've tried

not to sugarcoat the truth, even if
it hints at genocide,

at disasters

worsened by our actions. So the snowdrift
is the perfect place to conceal my first

response to his question. It's better to
be good, but not easier;

If we must

kill, we do; Faced with starvation, we chew
on what's edible, regardless of what's

lost. "For me, it's easier to be good,"
I tender, still

uncertain where I stood.

Childhoods End

Our apartment is full of children. They're not ours,
but we feed & clothe them, so
they work for us without pay. This arrangement
benefits everyone: Our milk grows
progressively cheaper, our beef more affordable,
our plastic accessories
numerous. My wife & I forget
the kids' names & origin stories, constantly ask
how they discovered us, if there's anything
not too complicated we could do
to help them. They're quiet, never staying
more than a few days,
cycling in & out of our living room,
our bedrooms & bathroom. When they mention
globalization, we strap on
noise-cancelling headphones blasting podcasts
about ordinary people like us. We desire
to be guiltless, to imagine a world
without borders, equality for all. The children
aren't supposed to pay
attention to their own feelings, wake up
& automatically punch in, repeat
each mindless chore 'til their joyless childhoods end.

You once felt gigantic

but are currently a grain of sand buried at the bottom of the sea,
are a fly on the windowpane

of a once-sacred mosque
lost in the heart of Christianity. Your glorious achievements

are scribbled footnotes on pages ripped from ancient tomes
subsequently set ablaze,

your manifestoes mistaken
as satire, as too eager to please. Your rightful place in history

is revised, the dates of your birth & death pushed aside
for more pressing memories.

Each song you composed
commences its inevitable process of decomposition,

each film you directed unable to witness its celluloid heroes
resurrected upon the screen,

all the streets named after you
ritualistically bulldozed, converted into numbered freeways.

You're the impenetrable fortress constructed by a civilization
that ceases to wage war,

the central star in a system
with no sentient creatures to imbue it with meaning.

Even the undiscerning worms crave better meat than yours,
will quickly forget this meal

you unwillingly feed them.

Jonathan Greenhause

Transferal

Deeds are scattered like rose petals across the pitted sidewalk,
are folded, crumpled, & scissored
into fantastical shapes, none of them signed or claimed
as they await the overtaxed embrace
of the burden of ownership. Collecting one after the other,
I jam my overstuffed pockets with the perforated dreams
of the recently jobless, suffocated
by ballooning mortgages, indebted to payday loans
whose terms are the serrated teeth of a mythological beast,
are the skin-tearing claws
of an unread clause. Their college degrees hang pointlessly
on the peeling walls of fortified homes
they've been forcefully evicted from, peace officers
escorting them out like pallbearers from the mortuary,
proud families reduced to the stare
of wounded animals expecting a scythe to slice through the air
& fell them like mercy.

Lost in a room
where you've never been,

you may be suffering from memory loss
or abandonment
or stuck in a dream from which

you can't awake.
You may be an older/younger version
of your better self

or disguised as someone else, unable
to spot the difference.
The walls begin to close in, or maybe

it's an optical illusion;
Maybe you're imagining this, thinking
you're reading a poem

about how you're lost in a room.
Upon the wall,
a clock's hands move backwards

'til you're shedding
the weight of your years. You search
behind the clock

for an escape route, since you believe
the room's a metaphor
for the life you're leading, or it's

a meeting place
for the inchoate, where possibility
flutters like a moth

Jonathan Greenhause

in moonlight, its wings trembling;
or, more likely,
this is just a room, & a poem's only

what we wish it to be,
even as we start to feel the walls
pressing up against us.

Not a Holocaust Poem

This is about happy thoughts, puppies, & golden fields of wheat;
& nothing's lurking in those fields,

no concealed message threatening to break
this peace & quiet, no serial killers stalking in the shadows;

& even the shadows are comforting, their darkness
offering forgetfulness & sleep.

No startling illnesses hide here,
no rising fevers incapable of being broken by antibiotics

or by buckets of ice; & these buckets of ice are only employed
to keep the champagne chilled

or to engage the curiosity
of the previously-mentioned puppies. No fiancées will vanish,

inexplicably stripped from us in a confusion of smoke & fire,
leaving us to make sense of lives

we must now live alone . . .
No, this isn't that kind of poem, & in these pages,

you'll meet the love of your life & live happily ever after
because this isn't a Holocaust poem,

no matter how much you fear
it'll become one, paranoid the next line is certain to bring

an improbable twist; Because when you get there,
it's just a box of puppies,

& you smile as you lift each one
& make believe this is really happening just as you wished it to.

Not for Sale

The minimum-wage worker drags the cart
packed with children, all of them
so cute, put together
so perfectly. Along the sidewalk cracks,
the wheels twist & pop, the ride
choppy. Occasionally,
couples stop him, ask how much
for the little girl with pigtails, for the boy
with the black eye. The worker
doesn't speak much English, struggles
to tell passersby these kids aren't for sale
'til tomorrow, & only
at the store itself, not illegally
like this, smack in the middle of the street.

A Makeshift Ark

I shelter several honeybees in my cupped palms, a makeshift ark
to guard them against CCD, against this shitstorm

of mites & pesticides & the steamrolling of their habitats.
They'll reside here 'til I discover how to feed them

with a modicum of pollen, a drink from dewdrops, sweat gathered
in my skin's lines & furrows. I'm careful

not to antagonize, one absentminded sting assuring their destruction,
my words honeyed, my lofty intentions

quick to take flight. All around us, colonies collapse, queen bees
reigning over ruins, abandoned hives bearing witness

to the tragedy of 10 million Roanokes. A lost world's in the works,
the bees' diaphanous wings clipped, their dried-out honeycombs

split apart. Even while writing this, my own home
splinters, the sea seeping in through the basement, my body

resting against the rotten planks of a rowboat;
&, for us, no gracious palms will be large enough to offer us flight.

Crystallized

An epidemic of loneliness, the doctor whispers in my ear
as I carve up pieces of braised short-ribs
at this high school reunion
for a school I didn't go to. She didn't either. We're
plus-ones chatting about statistics
of crystal meth overdoses, as a dessert tray's
replenished with chocolate chip cookies, then emptied,
replenished again. Outside,
ash floats like a swarm of moth stars. Coatless,
I clamber past ice sculptures into the cold
where a 40-something-year-old vomits into his wool hat
in the potholed parking lot, as I navigate
past Pabst cans, fumbling for my keys, teeth chattering,
breaths crystallizing into clouds
as nebulous as my teenage memories. Frosted oaks
inch closer, their invisible leaves
rustling like the brittle yellowed pages
of my long-gone English Lit class. Inside the hollows
of my passenger-side door, frozen water bottles
are a line of pissed-off seniors
pushing against plastic, ready to burst. *An epidemic
of loneliness*, I repeat, a prayer, lost
somewhere in time, alone like Ötzi, fingers trembling,
engine ignited, my wife screaming as she rushes to the car.

III. The Perfect Dad

Balloon

—After Anne Sexton's "Housewife"

Some men wed their stewing insecurities, ladle them
directly from the stove pot, then

miraculously stomach them, make cringe-worthy love
to their abominable mistakes,

sloppily French kissing their slovenly appearances
in the spotted looking glass,

lamenting their precipitousness since once resembling
Old School divinities. Theirs

is a bored game of settling for McMansion mediocrity,
a generic consolation prize

of skin-deep transgressions, ignoring their private itch
for Thoreau-like transcendence.

Their youthfulness: Liver-spotted. Ballooning desire's
dotted with pinpricks, a creaking tower

set to implode, as wives try blowing them back up
but are failure-bound. These men

are protein-supplement obsessives waging a forever war
with themselves, gung-ho soldiers

signing a suicide pact, scalded by smoldering fireworks
from their buried feelings,

are so estranged from their blissful amniotic beginnings,
they crave the buried placenta;

but they're no more the exalted Masters of their Domain
than a woman is every mother,

since each of these men is just himself, & just as lost.

The Perfect Dad

I'll be loving without spoiling, generous
without giving in, strict
without scarring, loads of fun
yet responsible, caring
but never smothering. I'll be that dad
everyone wishes could be hers or his,
not a caricature or phony,
not secretly raging or too wound up
to be authentic, not so perfect
that I'm not potentially on the verge
of a nervous breakdown. I'll play soccer
& baseball, badminton
& checkers, take the kids to circuses
stripped of their elephants,
to films screened at graveyards, hike,
& mail postcards composed
of clipped-out letters with vague clues
regarding our whereabouts. No one
will be able to locate us
while the kids are still minors,
their education a series of misadventures,
a misplaced sense of origin,
a fleeting belief that childhood's magical,
that their passionate dad
must realize what he's doing, why
I've slaughtered that cow
in a stranger's pasture
& now they're digging their hands
into its carcass, painting their faces red
with the warpaint of the dead,
why a squadron of police
are closing in, aiming directly at my chest.

Jonathan Greenhause

Domestic Poxes

A plague on your house,
         & mold, too.
Some misaligned beams

         & a colony
of carpenter ants, plus
         a reading

of radon in the basement.
         A sickness
laying low your sheetrock,

         a cheapening
of your resale value due
         to a rumor

of haunting, a hushed threat
         of eminent
domain. Paint warped,

         & a stain
dumped by rainstorms,
         A compromised

foundation, & a sump pump
         rendered
ineffective. A forked trail

         of invective
from envious neighbors;
         A color scheme

thwarted by a conspiracy
          of painters,
by a clique of unlicensed

          interior
decorators. Destabilizing
          tremors

culminating in disaster,
          in plastic pipes
set afire, in a sticky web

          of wrecked wires.
A pox on your house, & on
          your block, too,

on your neighborhood & each
          godforsaken
refuge you've ever sought.

How to Raise a Young Child

You're not certain what to feed your son today. Maybe
grasshoppers? Or Rice Krispies? Perhaps
a crocodile's appendix? Do
crocodiles even possess appendices? You haven't
fed your child today, yet you gift yourself
an hour to fill out postcards to faraway places. It's
almost the same. You watch
as your hair greys, as your son gnaws
at the peeling walls, scrapes wood shavings
from the floor, captures silverfish
& sticks them between his lips. Your son seems
joyous, so you leave the house,
let him raise himself. Kids require
independence. You return back home
several years later, rummage through the drawers
& discover him curled up
beside the hair-dryer. You apologize,
but he isn't upset, just pleads for spaghetti, wants you
to pretend it's monkey brains. You start sobbing
like you're supposed to, which means
uncontrollably. You feed him
lies, swear you'll always
be there for him, promise him this
seconds before slipping out through the back entrance.

My Sons & I

eat toasted butterflies,
scrambled
scarabs, poached cockroaches

& sautéed
caterpillars dotted with
ladybugs,

fatten ourselves on roasted
locusts,
munch on a mélange

of chiggers
& ticks baked in a crust
of mites,

of stir-fried silverfish.
We'd try
100% beef, but

the cow's
majestic, possesses
a soul

akin to ours, stares
queenlike
over her expanse

of prairies
& lends herself to verses
of epic

melancholy. We wax
bucolic,
figure we can fixate

on ants
covered in chocolate, on
arachnids

stuffed in puff pastries,
dig up
pill bugs & nightcrawlers,

swallow 'em
raw like oysters, like
steamed mussels,

hustle after bumblebees
& wasps,
stake out the resting spots

of moths,
of grasshoppers & fleas.
My wife's

a culinary *artiste*,
devises
a million ways to cook 'em,

advises
we travel more frequently
to marshlands,

arrive right at the dead
of night;
but our sons rebel, sneak out

to drive-thrus,
consume their bodyweight
in lamb,

slather themselves in Spam,
in lard, in
bacon grease. We increase

our sanctions
for disobedience, lock
their doors,

impose a diet of snails,
offer up
Millepiede Parmigiana

& kielbasa
ground from earthworms.
They squirm

through their upstairs windows,
zoom out
to a Sizzler's, wind up

bloated
in a KFC, discover
a slow pig

stranded by the highway,
tear it
to shreds, its bones scattered

across asphalt,
then they crawl back home,
bloodied hands

in prayer, as they swear
only insects
will cross their sacred lips.

Parabolic

We were never taught how to be parents, our children
thrust upon us like makeshift disasters,

held out as awkwardly as possible, their limbs
jutting in all directions;

& we, staring, awaited someone to mercifully
take them back. No one

ever takes them back: They scale us, disappointed
by their view on top, as if trekking

Mt. Everest's rubbish-strewn trails, their lofty idols
tainted by waste. Our majestic height's

inflated, then strip-mined by successive absences
at school plays, by our failure

to listen to the saccharine notes of their pop music.
Still, we carry on, clinging like grunts

upon our secret armory of language, must pinpoint
where we'll make the incision,

hopeful our loosened words might graze them
like butterflies briefly soaring,

like the parabolic rise of stones flung towards
the quivering slipshod wreck

of our distant homes. No one will ever love them
like we do: We lay ourselves down,

sacrificial slabs of splintered wood connecting tracks
as their trains rumble out of view.

The Trek North

This Spring, my two sons & I
march North, crossing
the Canadian border, sneaking
through gaps in pines. Ben
wears camouflage, paints his face
with mud; Samuel, asthmatic,
barely lifts his feet,
his breaths endangered species
cornered by altitude. Ben & I
fear Sam won't make it far;
but we shadow this illicit trail
of climate refugees
seeking the mercy of strangers.

Jonathan Greenhause

Damn Our Shortsightedness

I'm only semiconscious, body sunk into couch-cushions,
a maritime wreck barely breaching the surface

as my 6-year-old starts sobbing from where he sits
by his melted cup of ice cream, his tears

salt-tinged bullets splitting through my skin
as if by M16, as if that sadness

being quantifiable, if firmly held, might plunge my soul
into the molten belly of this Earth; & I know

I shouldn't laugh when he explains to me
between anguished gulps of air

that he's crying because he ate his ice cream too quickly
because he was afraid zombies

would break down our double-bolted front door
or climb through our 3rd-floor windows,

which—damn our shortsightedness—aren't boarded up
or outfitted with crossbows. I summon

all the courage I can as a thoughtful, caring parent
& successfully avoid laughing at this

for roughly a second or 2
before hopelessly succumbing to my insensitivity,

my sense of humor winning out
over the urge to comfort, even as I draw him towards me,

wrap him in my arms, & resist the natural temptation
to pretend to devour his brains.

Relics

I clutch this memory of my grandfather
stripped of his memory as if it were
a car radio & his rusted Lincoln
were the skull. We rest without music

at the penitentiary—or rather
his nursing home—its blank walls in need
of toddlers wielding crayons, of relics
arranged to read him back his history.

This was years ago. I stare at my father
& wonder if what I can't see begins
to vanish. The nurse extracts his IV,
says the storm will start soon, the winds

toppling walls like matchsticks, like memories
unanchored, at the mercy of the sea.

Jonathan Greenhause

Erich Kästner & the Lion's Jaws

Over the grinding of coffee beans & the boiling of water,
I strain to hear a scratchy recording of Erich Kästner

reciting his lines, this German songbird drowned out
by a lion's roar. In the living room, a pixelated iceberg

drifts towards my mesmerized children, their fates
like fledglings peering over the strawed edge. Below,

the city concrete is cracking, thaws & freezes,
then thaws again; as from that '60s auditorium, Kästner

describes his severed childhood in a metropolis
that's gone. My kids gaze at a different loss, our TV

birthing a world of pole-vaulting seas; meanwhile,
Kästner glides over a firebombed Dresden, recognizes

nothing. I recall my great-grandmother's village
near Łódź, Poland, hurriedly jot down "223,000 Jews"

on a flimsy napkin, then cross it off, replace it
with what now remains in the country, with "10,000";

then, the lion's jaws briefly stretch open, reveal
the same struggling songbird eagerly fluttering his wings.

Perfect

The boy wraps the dishrag 'round his head
so the cloth cascades down the sides
of his cheeks, like the girl's golden locks
he'd watched on TV, like the divine
Elsa, a Nordic
vision of perfection. His father
silently observes from the couch, thinks
what is right must always be
difficult, thus does it: He rises,
places his hands 'round the tilted dishrag
& carefully adjusts it, makes it
perfect.

Jonathan Greenhause

Goosenecks

You're at a State Park. To your right
is a barbeque grill
balanced on a pole hammered into

concrete & split rock.
To your left is your young son
joyously singing

"I nee-nee-need to see-see-see
my pá-pá-pá!"
But all you want to do

is write a poem
that, for once, isn't about wanting
to write a poem

about constantly being interrupted
by your young son;
& maybe—probably—you don't even

have a young son,
but I do. I'm on the other side of
this awkward dialogue,

& you're at your writing desk
or perhaps in bed,
while I'm at Goosenecks State Park

in Southern Utah,
struggling with a narrative shifting
from 2nd-person

to 1st, wondering why it is
that writing a poem
is sometimes so damn easy, yet

currently isn't.
I'm observing the macroscopic
geological carving

of this curving canyon, the tapered
layering of rock
etched by the San Juan River's

aqueous tongue
causing a natural collapse akin to
steppe pyramids:

Write back to me. Let me know
what you're seeing,
what marvels you've witnessed, who

you've seen develop
from fetus to 3-year-old, from parent
to ailing grandparent.

I want to know why sometimes
writing a poem
is so easy, yet being a parent is rife

with failure, with
a million unpardonable mistakes.
You'll find me here,

watching swallows dive-bombing
into the canyon,
then watching as they rise up again.

Jonathan Greenhause

Our Motel Amidst the Wildfire

An emergency broadcast floats upon soundwaves, the howl
of a wolfpack synchronized with our arthritic terrier

in her final days' repeating twilight. In a cracked painting,
clams nest by the jagged tideline, doubly accustomed

to daybreak & dusk. We invite the undying world, then expel it
like a zombie horde, my sons buried to their chins,

acrylic blankets wrapped around their aching skinniness,
a cot's springs whining as they set up camp

like gold-diggers, their sheets makeshift tents, pillows sundered
as feathers fill our unzipped suitcases,

our motel room a South-Atlantic isle splattered with guano,
the slim bright line blazing beneath our door

a single gill through which we breathe. Our hungover neighbor
conjures the motel manager, & we reason with him

that kids will be kids, overbearing even through an apocalypse.
3 blocks away, the sea somersaults, attacks stilts,

hankers for the crunch of coastal inhabitants. We grudgingly
pay the owed damages, our credit cards maxed,

our boys a mix of outlaw & do-gooder, of deciduous leaf
& choking vine. Just as the pop song swells

like a bellows mating with the blaze, it stutters & cuts, a voice
warning of a lynch mob, our asphalted links to home

severed by the march of brainwashed torch-bearing converts
ripping the future from our oil-slicked grasp.

Cradle

"The day which we fear as our last
is but the birthday of eternity."
–Lucius Annaeus Seneca

There will be Mylar balloons
& pointy hats with strings attached below the chin.
Party clowns (if that's your thing)
will perform magic tricks,
which you'll slickly solve on your own.
Your children (now grown) will ask if you'd like
another slice of pizza, of chocolate cake,
& you'll nod, sense your aching bones
growing limber & elastic. Your wrinkled skin
will stay wrinkled, & you'll feel a little silly
for having wished to tread them flat.
Your parents (long dead)
will lift you up, then cradle & rock you to sleep,
will usher you into a dream from which
you will never, ever awake.

A Foraging for Our Lost Fossils

Geese gaggle skyward as if crowding a concert hall, hollowed
bones echoing sainthood. What grave malice we bear

towards these raucous congregants, our avarice altering
their flight patterns, our curious missteps tourists

gored by bison. We repurpose our aviary & apiary colonies
as specters, rebrand the latter as honey's opposite,

as the flipside of sweet. In mudflats, my sons unearth treasure,
fossilized fangs a hush of stringless harps

that, if reinserted, would sink into calves & hens, into tender kids
as inquisitive as mine. Wading to their knees,

my boys lurch for perch, fists clenching the shutoff current
like twin cardinals unconsciously blessing

what no longer breathes, this fishy miracle of lessened bounties.
They wobble like sentient tops, immersed in waters

teeming with DDT's derivatives & Agent Orange's heirs,
the Earth's riches impoverished, as if pinned

after a sure-footed beast's spring crushing our bodies, their tails
windmilling in remembrance of what's gone.

Cupping Our Palms

Love is extending your cupped palms
to cradle the blend
of chewed-up pizza & clementines
in your 2-&-a-half-year-old's
sudden vomit, its warm acidity
stinging your fingers, dripping down
to the carpet below. Likely,
he won't remember this later in life
when you're proudly
beaming at his wedding, or when
he carefully guides you
back to your hospital bed, your gown
flapping open at the back;
but some subconscious piece of him
will vaguely recall,
will extend his own cupped palms
when the time comes to return the favor.

Jonathan Greenhause

About the Author

Jonathan Greenhause has won the Ledbury Poetry Competition, *Aesthetica Magazine*'s Creative Writing Award in Poetry, the Telluride Institute's Fischer Poetry Prize, and the *Prism Review* Poetry Prize, and his poems have appeared in *America, december, New York Quarterly, Notre Dame Review, Poetry Ireland Review, The Poetry Society, The Rialto, RHINO, Subtropics,* and the *Times Literary Supplement*. Jonathan lives in Jersey City with his wife and their two sons, all within a stone's throw of the local freight line.

jonathangreenhause.com

Acknowledgments

Versions of the following poems first appeared in these wonderful competitions, journals, magazines, and reviews:

America: "Thanks a lot, Shakespeare, for the Starling"
ArLiJo (Gival Press): "On the Road Trip"
Arts University Bournemouth International Poetry Prize: "Cupping Our Palms" and "Fireflies and Ice Cream"
Columbia Poetry Review: "How to Raise a Young Child"
december: "Goosenecks"
Fish Poetry Prize Anthology 2022: "The Perfect Dad"
Fourteen Hills: "Unwrapped"
Journal of New Jersey Poets: "Hit at the Jersey Shore"
Ledbury Poetry Competition: "The fire-escape, no longer weighed down"
The MacGuffin: "The Weight of Your Body"
Mick Imlah Poetry Prize (Times Literary Supplement): "Not for Sale"
Moon City Review: "A Makeshift Ark"
New Ohio Review: "You once felt gigantic"
Paterson Literary Review: "My father's across the Atlantic, on the verge"
The Plough Prize: "Domestic Poxes"
Poetry Ireland Review: "Beacons of Light"
The Poetry Society: "Animal House" and "To Sugarcoat the Truth"
Popshot: "Lost in a room where you've never been"
Potomac Review: "Damn Our Shortsightedness"
Reunion: "Relics"
The Rialto: "A poem written in my past life as a 15th-century Georgian monk"
Salamander: "Extant/Extinct"
Sugar House Review: "Not a Holocaust Poem"
Welsh Poetry Competition: "Circles"

Meadowlark POETRY

Books are a way to explore, connect, and discover. Poetry incites us to observe and think in new ways, bridging our understanding of the world with our artistic need to interact with, shape, and share it with others.

Publishing poetry is our way of saying—

We love these words,
we want to preserve them,
we want to play a role in sharing them
with the world.

Meadowlark Press
— since 2014 —

meadowlarkpoetrypress.com

Birdy Poetry Prize Winners

2021
Knowing Is a Branching Trail
Alison Hicks

"*Knowing is a Branching Trail* captured my attention. I read in search of moments that create a soft pause in me. Time given back to me that allows me to sit with feeling, safely and freely. There were voices in the work that transitioned from stranger to companion. It felt as if we shared an understanding. . . I felt less alone with this book."
–Huascar Medina, *Un Mango Grows in Kansas*

2020
Selected Poems: 2000-2020
JC Mehta

"With sharp and incisive language, each piece provides an immersive moment, inviting the reader into the experience of growing up half Cherokee, of self-harm and losing friends, of teaching and aging and loving and living in the Pacific Northwest. Nothing is veiled, nothing is alluded to, and their humor is ever-present, wry and witty."
–Brenna Crotty, Editor, *Selected Poems*

2019
A Certain Kind of Forgiveness
Carol Kapaun Ratchenski

"There is a worldliness in these poems, the kind of grit that accompanies a strong heart. There's awareness–of the self, of the world. And the poems are populated with the magical, husky things of this earth: warm beer in Berlin, rice in a bowl in a monastery, and stains from fresh cranberries. These are poems we can savor, now and again."
–Kevin Rabas, *More Than Words*

Meadowlark Press created The Birdy Poetry Prize to celebrate the voices of our era. Cash prize, publication, and 50 copies awarded annually.

Accepting Entries: September 1 - December 1

Entry Fee: $25

Prize: $1,000 cash, publication by Meadowlark Press, 50 copies of the completed book

All entries will be considered for standard Meadowlark publishing contract offers, as well.

Full-length poetry manuscripts (55 page minimum) will be considered. Poems may be previously published in journals and/or anthologies, but not in full-length single-author volumes. Poets are eligible to enter, regardless of publishing history.

See birdypoetryprize.com for complete submission guidelines. Also visit us at meadowlarkbookstore.com

Made in the USA
Middletown, DE
25 October 2022

13463222R00050